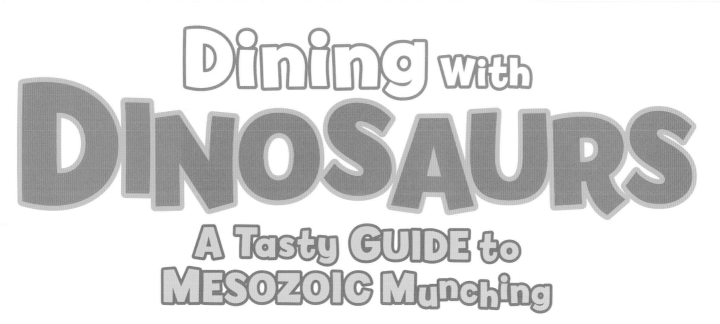

Dining with DINOSAURS
A Tasty GUIDE to MESOZOIC Munching

NATIONAL
GEOGRAPHIC
KiDS

WASHINGTON, D.C.

MEET THE "VORES"

WHO ATE WHO

Let's dive in! It's lunchtime and we're in China, in the Cretaceous period. This is where I'm from. The carnivores are busy chasing the herbivores, the herbivores both big and small are munching on plants, and the plants are chowing down on sunshine, air, water, and minerals—not your idea of a great meal, perhaps, but for a plant, it's better than ice cream.

Microraptor, a small feathered dinosaur

Jinzhousaurus, a dinosaur

Xianglong, a lizard

A **bennettite,** an extinct kind of plant

A **cycad,** a nonflowering plant

Eomaia, a mammal

Pycnophlebia, a grasshopper relative

MUNCH

Sinobaatar, a mammal

Trashivores in the soil and leaf litter

Dendrorhynchoides,
a pterosaur

Ginkgo,
a tree with stinky seeds

Euhelopus,
a dinosaur

Yutyrannus,
a dinosaur

Yanornis,
a bird

Jinzhousaurus,
a dinosaur

SCRUNCH!

Aeschnidium,
a dragonfly

Ephedra,
a nonflowering plant

Jeholornis, a bird
Yes, birds! Birds first appeared
in the Jurassic, so at this time
birds and other feathered
dinosaurs lived side by side.

GRAB!

Cretorabus,
a carnivorous beetle

Cretophasmomima,
a stick insect

THE MEGA CARNIVORES

We're going to start our "vores" tour with *T. rex* and company—the top predators of the dinosaur world. They hunted and ate big herbivores. Adult long-necks and armored plant-eaters may have been relatively safe, but any young or sick animal quickly became lunch. The mega carnivores were also happy to eat carrion, as we'll see on page 20.

HEAVENS, WHAT DREADFUL MANNERS! I DON'T KNOW WHY I BOTHERED TO BRING HER A KNIFE AND A FORK.

T. REX'S STEAK HOUSE
MENU

Starters:
Centrosaurus soup
Ankylosaur ankles

Main Courses:
Hadrosaur hash
Sauropod stew
Roast Triceratops
T-bone steak, T-rex style
Leptoceratops chops
Maiasaura mash

Note: We serve only free-range herbivores.

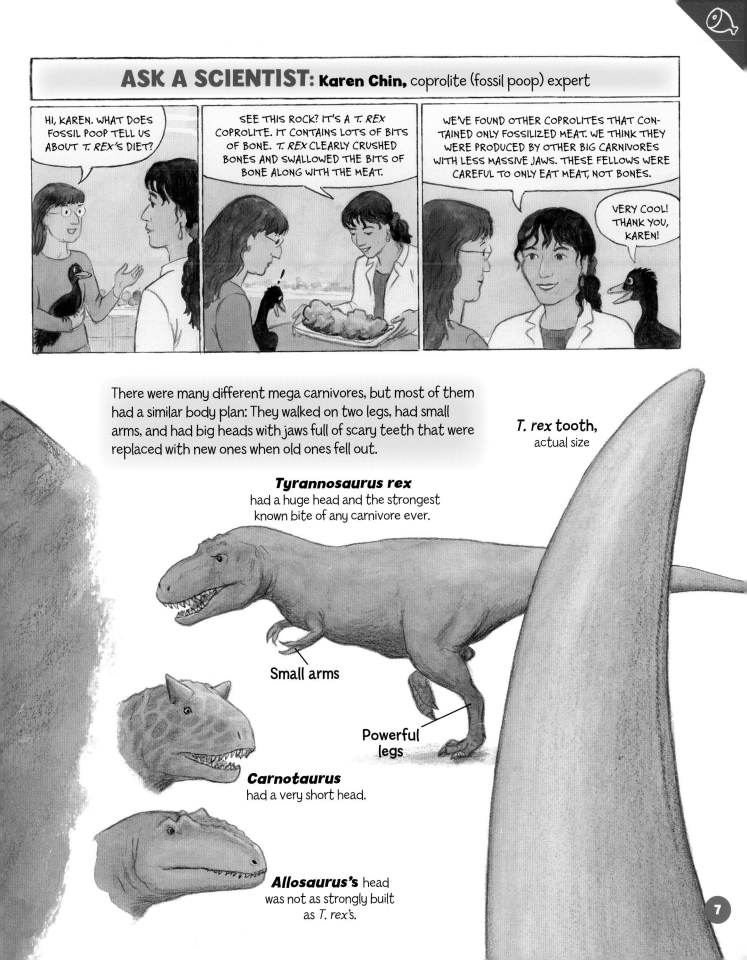

ASK A SCIENTIST: Karen Chin, coprolite (fossil poop) expert

HI, KAREN. WHAT DOES FOSSIL POOP TELL US ABOUT *T. REX'S* DIET?

SEE THIS ROCK? IT'S A *T. REX* COPROLITE. IT CONTAINS LOTS OF BITS OF BONE. *T. REX* CLEARLY CRUSHED BONES AND SWALLOWED THE BITS OF BONE ALONG WITH THE MEAT.

WE'VE FOUND OTHER COPROLITES THAT CONTAINED ONLY FOSSILIZED MEAT. WE THINK THEY WERE PRODUCED BY OTHER BIG CARNIVORES WITH LESS MASSIVE JAWS. THESE FELLOWS WERE CAREFUL TO ONLY EAT MEAT, NOT BONES.

VERY COOL! THANK YOU, KAREN!

There were many different mega carnivores, but most of them had a similar body plan: They walked on two legs, had small arms, and had big heads with jaws full of scary teeth that were replaced with new ones when old ones fell out.

T. rex tooth, actual size

Tyrannosaurus rex had a huge head and the strongest known bite of any carnivore ever.

Small arms

Powerful legs

Carnotaurus had a very short head.

Allosaurus's head was not as strongly built as *T. rex's*.

THE RAPTORS: MIDSIZE PREDATORS

These guys were smaller and less powerfully built than the mega carnivores, so they couldn't use brute force to hunt. Instead they used their agility, their wits, and a wicked-sharp set of teeth and talons. When going after big herbivores, they hunted in packs.

The **raptors** had a larger brain in relation to their body than most of the other dinosaurs.

Their **sharp teeth** had ridges, like a steak knife.

Deinonychus

Deinonychus **tooth,** actual size

The largest **talon** was kept raised up when not in use.

The raptors couldn't fly, but **feathered arms** may have been used for display, for keeping their balance during an attack, and for protecting eggs in the nest.

This is what we thought *Deinonychus* looked like before the discovery of fossils that showed that many raptors and other dinosaurs had feathers.

MINI CARNIVORES AND OMNIVORES

This is my page! I'm a mini carnivore, and I'm not picky: I munch on birds, fish, lizards, small mammals, and even the occasional bug. I like to call myself a "whatever-I-can-catchivore."

Microraptor,
a crow-size dinosaur that glided on four wings

Sinosauropteryx,
a small dinosaur

Gobiconodon,
a possum-size mammal

This **Microraptor** fossil includes fish bones from its last meal. Other *Microraptor* fossils have been found with mammal, bird, and lizard remains in them.

Fish bones

Mei,
another small dinosaur

I GUESS MICRO AND I HAVE A LOT IN COMMON!

Felis,
a modern mini carnivore

I ATE ALL SORTS OF THINGS. DOES THAT MEAN I'M AN OMNIVORE, WHICH MEANS "EVERYTHING-EATER"?

ACTUALLY, NO. OMNIVORES EAT BOTH ANIMALS AND PLANTS. AS FAR AS WE KNOW, YOU ATE ONLY ANIMALS.

HOW CAN YOU TELL WHICH ANIMALS WERE OMNIVORES?

TEETH THAT ARE GOOD FOR EATING BOTH MEAT AND PLANTS ARE OUR MOST IMPORTANT CLUE, AS WELL AS THE SHAPE OF THE SKULL AND BODY, BUT WE CAN'T ALWAYS BE SURE.

Citipati belonged to a group of omnivorous dinosaurs from Mongolia and China called oviraptorosaurs.

Some dinosaurs were true omnivores. Others were omnivorous only on occasion: Baby herbivores probably got extra protein by adding bugs and small animals to their diet, and some small carnivores may have snacked on seeds and fruit from time to time. And like blackbirds and robins today, some Mesozoic birds probably ate a mix of berries, seeds, worms, and insects.

Citipati's **parrot-like beak** could have been used to crush hard seeds and plants or to snap up small animals.

Twenty million years in the future, scientists from another galaxy discover a fossil of a human.

FLAT FRONT TEETH AND CHEWING-TYPE MOLARS—I SAY IT WAS AN HERBIVORE!

YEAH, BUT THE EYES FACE FORWARD LIKE A PREDATOR'S, AND IT HAS A HUGE BRAIN. MAYBE IT HUNTED IN WELL-ORGANIZED PACKS.*

* Both are true: We're omnivores!

THE INSECTIVORES

I prefer to call these critters "buggivores" (which is a made-up name) because I like how it sounds, and because insectivores also eat spiders, centipedes, and other creepy-crawlies that aren't insects. Bugs are delicious, by the way—you should try some!

The creatures sharing the feast below all lived in China in the Jurassic and Cretaceous periods.

Dendrorhynchoides, a pterosaur

MY ABSOLUTE FAVORITES ARE SMALL BEETLES. HOW ABOUT YOU?

Eomaia, a mammal

TOO CRUNCHY. I PREFER SQUISHY GRUBS.

Jeholodens, a mammal

Eoenantiornis, a bird

Liaobatrachus, a frog

AREN'T WE REALLY A KIND OF CARNIVORE?

Liaoxitriton, a salamander

YOU BET! WE EAT BUG MEAT!

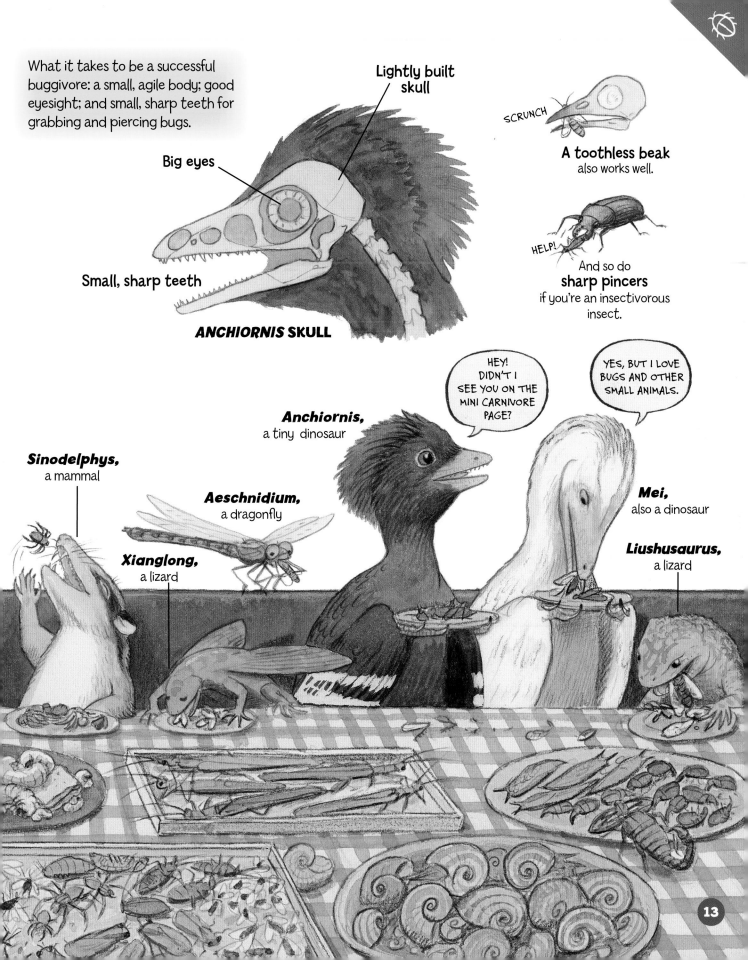

What it takes to be a successful buggivore: a small, agile body; good eyesight; and small, sharp teeth for grabbing and piercing bugs.

Lightly built skull

Big eyes

Small, sharp teeth

ANCHIORNIS SKULL

SCRUNCH

A toothless beak
also works well.

HELP!

And so do
sharp pincers
if you're an insectivorous insect.

HEY! DIDN'T I SEE YOU ON THE MINI CARNIVORE PAGE?

YES, BUT I LOVE BUGS AND OTHER SMALL ANIMALS.

Anchiornis,
a tiny dinosaur

Sinodelphys,
a mammal

Aeschnidium,
a dragonfly

Xianglong,
a lizard

Mei,
also a dinosaur

Liushusaurus,
a lizard

THE PISCIVORES

The piscivores (pronounced PIH-si-vors) are fish-eaters. Let's meet some piscivores that lived in North Africa in the Cretaceous. Today this area is a desert, but in the Cretaceous it was full of rivers and lakes, and the fishing was excellent.

Coloborhynchus, a pterosaur

Spinosaurus was an enormous dinosaur: just under 50 feet (15 m) long, which is quite a bit longer than *T. Rex.*

Mawsonia, a coelacanth
Huge fish like *Mawsonia* provided the megameals that allowed *Spinosaurus* to get so big.

Ceratodus, a lungfish

Elosuchus, a crocodile

ASK A SCIENTIST:
Nizar Ibrahim, paleontologist and National Geographic Explorer

HELLO, NIZAR. HOW CAN YOU TELL THAT THESE ANIMALS ATE FISH?

SEE THESE LONG, NARROW JAWS AND POINTY, CONE-SHAPED TEETH? THEY'RE PERFECT FOR GRABBING SLIPPERY FISH.

Crocodile skull

Pterosaur skull

Spinosaurus skull

ALSO, BOTH SPINOSAURUS AND THE CROCODILE HAVE LITTLE PITS ON THEIR SNOUTS. IN MODERN ALLIGATORS, PITS JUST LIKE THESE CONTAIN PRESSURE SENSORS FOR LOCATING PREY UNDERWATER.

Sensory pits

SPINY'S NOSTRILS ARE ANOTHER CLUE: THEY'RE HIGH UP ON THE SKULL, SO SPINY COULD PUT ITS SNOUT UNDERWATER WITHOUT GETTING WATER UP ITS NOSE.

DID LOTS OF DIFFERENT DINOSAURS EAT FISH?

NOT AT ALL! ONLY A HANDFUL OF DINOSAURS BECAME PISCIVORES, AND THEY WERE ALL RELATIVES OF SPINOSAURUS, SUCH AS BARYONYX AND IRRITATOR.

THANKS, NIZAR!

Spinosaurus
50 feet (15 m)

Elosuchus
26 feet (8 m)

Onchopristis
25 feet (7 m)

Coloborhynchus
Wingspan 16 feet
(almost 5 m)

Compact car
14 feet (4.3 m)

Mawsonia
13 feet (4 m)

Onchopristis,
a sawfish
(a member of
the ray family)

WHO ATE WHO: IN THE OCEAN

A "Who Ate Who" of the oceans could fill an entire book. Here is just a taste of what was on the menu in the salty seas. What was NOT on the menu were dinosaurs: Strangely enough, except for some seabirds, no other dinosaurs took to the sea, but there were plenty of big marine reptiles instead.

These creatures all lived in what is now Kansas. Yes, in Kansas! In the Cretaceous, the sea covered the entire middle part of North America.

Just like today, the main food-makers in the oceans were tiny micro-sunivores called **phytoplankton** (pronounced FIE-toe-PLANK-ton). Zillions of these micro-sunivores turned air, water, and sunlight into food for the rest of the ocean food web to eat, the same way plants do on land.

Tiny animals called **zooplankton** (pronounced ZOO-oh-PLANK-ton) ate the phytoplankton. They were and still are the ocean's main herbivores.

Tiny crustacean

Fish eggs

Baby jellyfish

Fish larva

Seaweed also makes food using sunlight.

MUNCH! MUNCH!

Pteranodon,
a pterosaur with a wingspan of
up to 23 feet (7 m)

Ichthyornis,
a gull-like seabird

Hesperornis,
a big, flightless bird

Protostega,
a turtle

Tylosaurus,
a mosasaur

An **ammonite,** a
shelled relative of squid
Some ammonites were
predators; others ate plankton.

Marine **reptiles** and
sharks were the top
predators.

Squid

Styxosaurus,
a plesiosaur

Clams
filtered small bits of food
from the water.

Bonnerichthys,
a giant fish that strained
plankton from the water

THE DINOVORES

I'LL HAVE THE SAUROPOD STEW, PLEASE.

The main predators of dinosaurs were, of course, other dinosaurs. But it turns out that dinosaurs also had quite a few non-dinosaur enemies to worry about. Who were these "dinovores"? You'll discover a bunch of them below!

LARGEST
Two different crocodiles, **Deinosuchus** and **Sarcosuchus,** were almost as long as a *T. rex* and besides eating fish probably caught any unwary dino at water's edge.

CROC-INFESTED WATERS
NO SWIMMING

Deinosuchus

STRANGEST
A big snake called **Sanajeh** was buried and fossilized just as it was about to eat a newly hatched sauropod!

DO I HEAR HISSING?

SMALLEST

①

Fossil fleas

SCRATCH! SCRATCH!

They were large (for fleas) and probably lived on feathered dinosaurs. They were about one inch (2.5 cm) long.

②

A microscopic parasite

Scientists have found *T. rex* fossils with signs of an infection that is very similar to one that infects birds today.

POSSIBLE "DINOVORE"

Beelzebufo, a toad from Madagascar, grew up to 16 inches (40 cm) long and it *might* have included newly hatched dinosaurs in its diet.

GRRRRRRRRRRRIBITT!

FURRIEST

Most Mesozoic mammals were small, but not all! **Repenomamus** was about the size of a badger. One *Repenomamus* fossil had the remains of a baby dinosaur called **Psittacosaurus** in its stomach.

Repenomamus fossil

Psittacosaurus remains

MICRO, IT JUST OCCURRED TO ME THAT WHEN I EAT CHICKEN OR TURKEY, I'M REALLY EATING A DINOSAUR!

GOOD GRIEF, YOU'RE A DINOVORE, TOO!

THE SCAVENGERS: DEAD DINO FOR DINNER

Meat is full of nutritious protein, but it's hard to catch. The reason is obvious: If you saw a hungry-looking carnivore approaching, you would run away as fast as you could, too. No one likes to get eaten! This is why most predators are happy to also eat carrion, meaning an animal that's already dead. Carrion may be stinky, but it's really easy to catch.

T. rex had a good sense of smell, which helped it find rotting carrion.

Two **Tyrannosaurus rex** are ripping off chunks of meat. We don't know if *T. rex* ate side by side like this, or whether the biggest *T. rex* chased the other scavengers away.

Alamosaurus could weigh more than 88,000 pounds (40,000 kg) —that's a lot of food!

A **raptor** joins the fun, making sure not to get too close to the *T. rex*.

TYRANNO TAKES A TRIP TO THE **GROSS**ERY STORE

TODAY'S SPECIAL: ROTTEN RIBS $6.00/lb

MAY I HELP YOU?

YES. 400 POUNDS OF STINKY STEAK, PLEASE!

PUTRID POT PIE

MAGGOT MUFFINS

HORRIBLE HAM

RAUNCHY ROAST

ROTTEN RIBS

STINKY STEAK

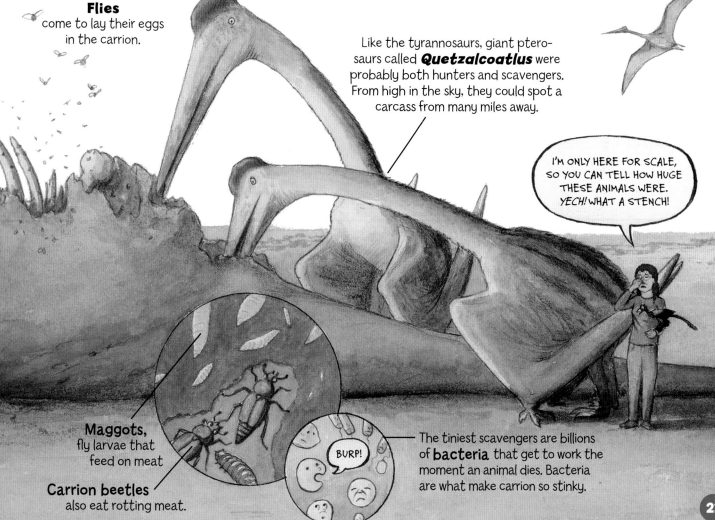

Flies come to lay their eggs in the carrion.

Like the tyrannosaurs, giant pterosaurs called **Quetzalcoatlus** were probably both hunters and scavengers. From high in the sky, they could spot a carcass from many miles away.

I'M ONLY HERE FOR SCALE, SO YOU CAN TELL HOW HUGE THESE ANIMALS WERE. YECH! WHAT A STENCH!

Maggots, fly larvae that feed on meat

BURP!

Carrion beetles also eat rotting meat.

The tiniest scavengers are billions of **bacteria** that get to work the moment an animal dies. Bacteria are what make carrion so stinky.

THE MEGA HERBIVORES

Diplodocus

Now on to the herbivores. Plants are a great source of food. They're nutritious, there are lots of them, and they can't run away! No wonder so many different kinds of dinosaurs became vegetarians. The largest herbivores of all were the sauropods, or long-necks. Let's take a look at how these giants got so big on a diet of nothing but greenery.

The **skull** was very lightweight.

No **chewing teeth**— *Diplodocus* swallowed without chewing.

The **front teeth** formed a rake to strip leaves off twigs.

—— **Conifers** (relatives of modern pines, cypresses, and monkey puzzles)

Horsetails

Ferns

Thanks to their **long necks,** these giants could stand in one spot and reach food on the ground, in shrubs, and high up in the trees. They saved lots of energy by moving their enormous bodies less often.

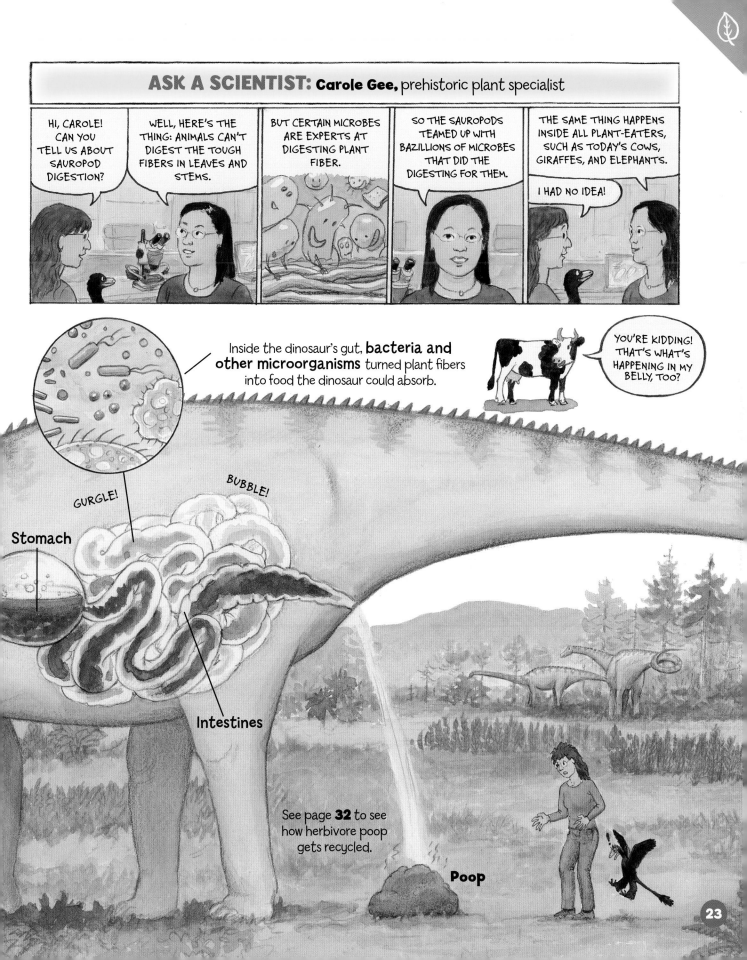

THE CHEEKY CHEWERS

Check out the crowd at this vegetarian supermarket. There's every possible size and shape of herbivores, but they all have one thing in common: They chewed their food before swallowing it. Food that's been broken into little bits is easier to digest, especially for gut microbes.

All the dinosaurs we've seen until now have been saurischians (pronounced saw-RISS-kee-ans). The dinos we see here belong to the other big branch of the dinosaur family tree, the ornithischians (orr-ni-THISS-kee-ans). The ornithischians were all plant-eaters.

Horny beak
for snipping off leaves and stems

Rows of **chewing teeth**
for grinding plant matter

TIMELESS FAVORITES : NONFLOWERING PLANTS

HERBOMART: THE

YE

FERNS

Maiasaura

TENDER GREENS

ARAUCARIA

Saurolophus

Sauropelta

Stegosaurus

GINKGO

These dinosaurs had cheeks to keep their food in place while they were chewing it. We humans have nice fleshy cheeks for the same reason. You wouldn't be able to chew gum without them!

PLENTY MORE
PLANT-EATERS

Check out this bizarre assortment of veggie-eaters! Besides the long-necks and the chewers, various other groups of dinosaurs also took to eating plants. So did many of the mammals and reptiles that shared their world. These are just a few examples. Large animals like *Nothronychus* had big bellies for digesting piles of leaves (with the help of microbes, of course). Many small herbivores preferred seeds, berries, and tender shoots, which concentrate more nutrition in a small package.

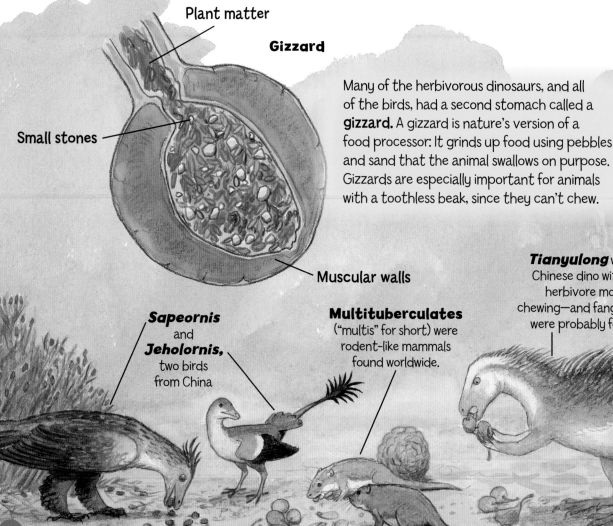

Plant matter

Gizzard

Small stones

Muscular walls

Many of the herbivorous dinosaurs, and all of the birds, had a second stomach called a **gizzard.** A gizzard is nature's version of a food processor: It grinds up food using pebbles and sand that the animal swallows on purpose. Gizzards are especially important for animals with a toothless beak, since they can't chew.

Tianyulong was a small Chinese dino with typical herbivore molars for chewing—and fangs! The fangs were probably for display.

Sapeornis and ***Jeholornis,*** two birds from China

Multituberculates ("multis" for short) were rodent-like mammals found worldwide.

Nothronychus,
a sloth-like dinosaur that
lived in North America

Struthiomimus was an
ostrich-like dinosaur with a toothless
beak. And like an ostrich, it most
likely ate seeds, fruit, and greenery. It
lived in what is now Canada.

Leaellynosaura,
a dinosaur from Australia

Simosuchus,
a vegetarian mini-croc
from Madagascar

TINY HERBIVORES, BIG APPETITES

Insects may be tiny compared to dinosaurs, but there were LOTS of them, and they had BIG appetites. They had hundreds of ways of munching on plants or sucking up their juices. Some insects helped pollinate plants in exchange for eating some of the pollen or sipping sweet liquid provided by the plant.

For most of dino history the plants were all nonflowering plants. Instead of flowers, some plants had cones that were pollinated by insects. This cone belongs to a cycad.

A **grasshopper** chomps on a leaf edge.

SCRUNCH!
SCRUNCH!

HOW LEAF ERICSON CONQUERED GREEN LAND BY HERB IVORE

MUNCH!

A **true bug** (a kind of insect with piercing mouthparts) dines on plant juice.

Tiny **moth larvae** munch tunnels inside a leaf.

Flowering plants became common in the second half of the Cretaceous, and many new pollinating insects appeared.

A **butterfly** ancestor feeds on an early flower.

A **scorpion fly** sips sweet liquid from a conifer cone.

THE SUNIVORES: PLANTS

I made up the name "sunivores" for the plants because plants use the energy of the sun to turn water and air into food. Sounds like magic, doesn't it? It's called photosynthesis, and if you want to see the recipe, it's on page 37. Thanks to this magic, plants and their ocean equivalents are the food factory for the entire planet. Everyone either eats a plant, eats a plant-eater, or eats someone who ate a plant-eater. Without plants, there would be no food web.

Sunshine
SPA AND CAFÉ

BEVERAGES FOR HAPPY ROOTS:

Nutriwater $4.00
Compost tea $5.00
Root beer $3.00
Mineral water $2.00
Cup o' dirt broth $1.50

HIGH-ENERGY SNACKS:

20 minutes strong sunlight $7.00
40 minutes regular sunlight $8.00
30 minutes sunlight
  with aromatherapy $8.50
Spritz of CO_2 $1.50
Double spritz of CO_2 $2.75

Sunshine Spa ROOT SOAK

Conifers

Cycads

Ferns

Moss

Nonflowering plants ruled for most of the Mesozoic.

In the Mid-Cretaceous, flowering plants became common.

Flowering plants ruled in the Late Cretaceous.

THE TRASHIVORES: DINING ON DUNG

Trashivores is a name we made up for nature's recyclers. A pile of dino poop? A dead pterosaur? A fallen tree? Piles of leaves? No problem! The trashivores are here to help! The trashivores eat dead plant and animal matter and complete the food web by converting all this waste into nutrients that they return to the soil.

Maiasaura, a duck-billed dinosaur

Pile of Maiasaura dung (Dung is the polite name for animal poop.)

Certain **fungi** specialize in recycling dung.

Earthworms help mix organic matter into the soil.

The most important decomposers of all are billions and billions of **bacteria.** They free up the nutrients that plants need to grow.

ASK A SCIENTIST: We go back to see **Karen Chin,** coprolite (fossil poop) expert.

HI, KAREN! HAVE YOU ALSO STUDIED HERBIVORE POOP?

I HAVE! I STUDIED *MAIASAURA* COPROLITES AND FOUND DUNG BEETLE TUNNELS IN THEM.

DUNG BEETLES ARE EXTREMELY IMPORTANT TODAY FOR RECYCLING MAMMAL DUNG. WITHOUT THEM IT WOULD PILE UP AND BE A HUGE PROBLEM.

IT WAS EXCITING TO DISCOVER THAT BEETLES EVOLVED AN APPETITE FOR DUNG LONG BEFORE BIG MAMMALS APPEARED ON THE SCENE.

Flies flock to lay their eggs in the dung.

There are two kinds of trashivores: **detritivores,** which are animals that feed on bits and pieces of dead organic matter, and **decomposers,** which are bacteria and fungi that take the final step of freeing up the nutrients that plants need to grow.

Close-up of **maggots** (fly larvae)

A fungus called **white rot** breaks down wood, making it soft and nutritious enough for *Maiasaura* to munch on.

Dung beetles move dung underground, where it fertilizes the soil.

Dung beetle egg

Close-up of a **beetle** packing dung into a tunnel to lay its egg in

Mites and other tiny invertebrates munch on dead plants and fungi.

WHO EATS WHO TODAY?

This scene looks familiar, doesn't it? Today we have all the same "vores" as in the Mesozoic, only the big predators and herbivores are mammals instead of dinosaurs because those dinosaurs went extinct. The small feathered dinosaurs we call birds are very much still alive, though.

Enjoy your 21st-century food web, dear omnivore, and be good and eat your broccoli!

THE FOOD WEB

A food web is the combination of all the connections between the different "vores." The sunivores are called producers because they make, or produce, food. The rest are called consumers because they eat (consume) food instead of making it.

One way we can think of the food web is like a pyramid ... or a layer cake! Each level of the cake uses lots of energy and passes only a small amount on up to the next level, which is why there are lots of sunivores, fewer herbivores, and even fewer carnivores.

CARNIVORES

are **SECONDARY CONSUMERS.** They're the icing on the cake.

FEW CARNIVORES

HERBIVORES

are **PRIMARY CONSUMERS.** They're the rich top layer.

A **BUNCH** of HERBIVORES

SUNIVORES

are **PRODUCERS.** They're the main part of the cake.

LOTS of SUNIVORES

TRASHIVORES

are the base of the cake. They recycle everything so nutrients aren't lost.

A **BUNCH** of TRASHIVORES

PHOTOSYNTHESIS

Recipe: SUGAR FROM SUNSHINE

From the kitchen of: THE SUNIVORES

Ingredients:

6 molecules of H_2O
(water, pulled up from roots)

6 molecules of CO_2
(carbon dioxide, taken up from the air)

Sunlight

You will also need:

ATP molecules, which are like tiny rechargeable batteries

Enzymes, which are proteins that can assemble or pull apart other molecules

Chlorophyll, a green light-catching pigment in the chloroplasts

Directions:

Put your chlorophyll in the sun so it can soak up energy. Add the water and enzymes, and stir well. The water molecules will come apart and the oxygen atoms will float away in pairs.

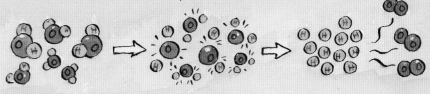

Combine the 12 hydrogen atoms from the water with the 6 carbon dioxide molecules, a big pack of enzymes, and the ATP (the ATP provides the energy to glom it all together), and you have **sugar!**

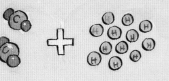 

This kind of sugar is called **GLUCOSE,** and it has a formula of $C_6H_{12}O_6$.

FUN WITH GLUCOSE

Here are some of the things that plants can do with glucose:

1. Burn the glucose in their cells to get energy. Animals do this too. It's called cellular respiration.

2. Change the glucose into a different kind of sugar (for example, fructose, one of the main sugars in fruit).

3. Turn it into fibers to support their bodies. Cellulose is the main fiber in plant leaves and stems, and lignin is the fiber that makes wood so strong.

4. Store it for later in the form of starch (think potatoes, wheat, or corn) or oils like those in almonds or olives.

Incredibly, all these things, from the sweetness of a peach to the trunk of a sequoia, are made from just the simple building blocks of glucose: carbon, oxygen, and hydrogen. But in order to make proteins and all sorts of other things, the plant needs nitrogen, phosphorous, and many other nutrients, which it gets from the soil.

Shopping list:
3 bags of bugs
Pine nuts
2 lbs ginkgo nuts
stegosaurus steak
candy

SOME NOTES FROM HANNAH

MORE ON THE "VORES"

The suffix (word ending) "-vore" comes from the Latin *vorare*, "to devour." Besides the ones in the book, scientists use quite a few more "-vore" names. These are some examples:

Faunivore is another word for "carnivore" ("fauna" means all the animals that live in a particular environment).
Folivores eat leaves.
Frugivores eat fruit.
Fungivores eat fungi.
Planktivores eat plankton.
Spongivores eat sponges.
Vermivores eat worms.

OTHER FOOD WEB TERMS you may come across are **"autotroph,"** which means the same thing as "producer" (the word "autotroph" means "self-feeding" in Greek), and the **"heterotroph"** ("other-fed" in Greek), which is the same thing as "consumer." I mention only primary and secondary consumers on the food web cake, but you might also see the term "tertiary consumer" for a carnivore that eats other carnivores, and there can even be "quaternary consumers"—for instance, an orca that eats salmon that eat smaller fish that in turn eat zooplankton.

THE PALEO-ENVIRONMENTS IN THE BOOK

"Who Ate Who" on pages 4-5 takes place in a fossil area in northeast China known as the Jehol Group. Jehol fossils preserve incredibly fine details, including feathers and fur, and have proved that many dinosaurs had feathers. The mini carnivores on page 10 and most of the insectivores on pages 12-13 are also from the Jehol.

The piscivore scene on pages 14-15 takes place in Morocco, in a fossil-rich area called the Kem Kem beds. Today, this area of the Sahara is bone-dry (ha ha), but it was a large river system during the Mesozoic era.

The ocean scene on pages 16-17 is set in the Cretaceous Interior Seaway, which covered the central part of North America. The land on either side was home to the chewing herbivores on pages 24-25 (except for *Stegosaurus*, which is from the Jurassic period). *T. rex* and company on the "Dead Dino for Dinner" pages (20-21) are from the very end of the Cretaceous period. *Diplodocus* on page 22 was also from North America but lived earlier, in the Jurassic. It comes from a series of dinosaur-rich rock layers called the Morrison formation.

Find out more at **hannahbonner.com.**

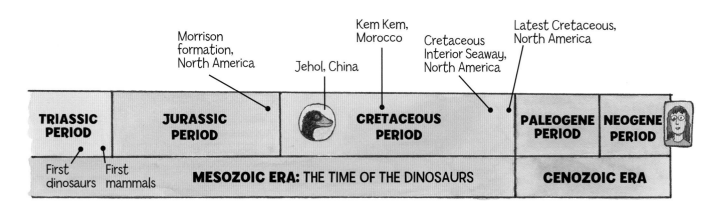

Morrison formation, North America

Jehol, China

Kem Kem, Morocco

Cretaceous Interior Seaway, North America

Latest Cretaceous, North America

| TRIASSIC PERIOD | JURASSIC PERIOD | | CRETACEOUS PERIOD | PALEOGENE PERIOD | NEOGENE PERIOD |

First dinosaurs   First mammals

MESOZOIC ERA: THE TIME OF THE DINOSAURS

CENOZOIC ERA

How to pronounce the scientific names in this book

NOTE: The pronunciations are in American English. Some of these names are pronounced differently in British English.

Aeschnidium (ay-SKNID-ee-um)

Alamosaurus (al-uh-mo-SAWR-us)

Allosaurus (al-o-SAWR-us)

ammonite (AM-oh-nite)

Anchiornis (an-kee-OR-nis)

Ankylosaur (an-KY-lo-sawr)

Baryonyx (barry-ON-ix)

Beelzebufo (BEE-el-ze-BOOF-oh)

bennettite (BEN-ne-tite)

Bonnerichthys (bon-er-IK-theez) ("th" as in thistle)

Carnotaurus (kar-noh-TOHR-us)

Cenozoic (sen-oh-ZO-ik)

Centrosaurus (sen-truh-SAWR-us)

Ceratodus (ser-a-TOAD-us)

chlorophyll (KLOR-uh-fil)

Citipati (SIT-uh-pah-tee)

coelacanth (SEE-luh-canth)

Coloborhynchus (co-LOW-buh-RINK-us)

Cretaceous (kre-TAY-shus)

wCretophasmomima (cret-oh-FASS-moh-MY-mah)

Cretorabus (cree-toh-RAY-bus)

Deinonychus (dy-NON-i-kuss)

Deinosuchus (dy-noh-SOO-kuss)

Dendrorhynchoides (den-dro-rin-KOY-dees)

detritivore (de-TRY-ti-vor)

Diplodocus (dip-LOD-uh-kus or DIP-low-DOCK-us)

Elosuchus (ee-loh-SOO-kus)

Eoenantiornis (ee-oh-in-ant-tee-OR-nis)

Eomaia (ee-oh-MY-ah)

Ephedra (e-FEH-druh)

Euhelopus (yoo-hel-OH-puss)

fungi (FUN-guy or FUNJ-eye)

ginkgo (GHIN-koe)

Gobiconodon (go-bee-CON-o-don)

Hadrosaur (HAD-ruh-sawr)

Hesperornis (hess-per-OR-niss)

Ichthyornis (ik-thee-OR-nis)

Irritator (ih-ri-TAY-tor)

Jeholodens (jay-HOL-o-dens)

Jeholornis (jay-hol-OR-niss)

Jinzhousaurus (jin-zhoo-SAWR-us) ("zh" like the "s" in treasure)

Jurassic (jur-ASS-ik)

Leaellynosaura (LAY-el-in-a-SAWR-a)

Leptoceratops (lep-toe-SER-ah-tops)

Liaobatrachus (LEE-ow-bah-TRAY-kus) ("ow" as in cow)

Liaoxitriton (LEE-ow-shee-TRY-ton)

Liushusaurus (lee-oo-shoo-SAWR-us)

Maiasaura (my-ah-SAWR-ah)

Mawsonia (maw-SOE-nee-ah)

Mei (MAY)

Mesozoic (meh-zuh-ZO-ik)

Microraptor (my-crow-RAP-tor)

Neogene (NEE-oh-jeen)

Nothronychus (noth-roh-NY-kus)

Onchopristis (on-koe-PRISS-tis)

Oviraptorosaurs (oh-vih-rap-TAW-ro-sawrz)

Paleogene (PAY-lee-oh-jeen)

Pentaceratops (pent-ah-SER-ah-tops)

piscivore (PIH-si-vor)

Protostega (pro-toe-STAY-gah)

Psittacosaurus (sih-TAK-uh-SAWR-us)

Pteranodon (ter-RAN-o-don)

Pycnophlebia (pik-no-FLEE-bee-ah)

Quetzalcoatlus (KET-zuhl-ko-AT-lus)

Repenomamus (reh-pen-oh-MAM-us)

Sanajeh (sa-NAH-jeh)

Sapeornis (say-pee-OR-nis)

Sarcosuchus (sark-oh-SOO-kus)

Saurolophus (sawr-oh-LOAF-us)

Sauropelta (sawr-oh-PEL-ta)

sauropod (SAWR-uh-pod)

Saurornitholestes (sawr-OR-nith-oh-LEST-eez)

Simosuchus (sy-mo-SOO-kus)

Sinobaatar (SY-no-bah-tar)

Sinodelphys (sy-noe-DEL-fis)

Sinosauropteryx (sy-no-sawr-OP-ter-ix)

Spinosaurus (SPINE-oh-SAWR-us)

Stegoceras (steh-GAH-ser-us)

Stegosaurus (steg-oh-SORE-us)

Struthiomimus (struth-ee-oh-MY-mus)

Styxosaurus (stick-so-SAWR-uhs)

Tenontosaurus (teh-NON-tah-SAWR-us)

Tianyulong (tee-AN-yu-long)

Triassic (try-ASS-ik)

Triceratops (try-SERRA-tops)

Tylosaurus (ty-luh-SAWR-uhs)

Tyrannosaurus rex (tie-RAN-oh-SAWR-us rex)

Velociraptor (vel-OSS-ih-rap-tor)

Xianglong (shee-AHNG-long)

Yanornis (yah-NOR-niss)

Yutyrannus (yoo-ty-RAN-us)

Glossary of words not defined in the text

bacterium: (plural: bacteria) A kind of cell that is smaller and simpler than the cells of animals, fungi, and plants.

bug: In this book "bug" is used in the popular sense of insects as well as other invertebrates such as spiders, centipedes, and worms.

carcass: The body of a dead animal.

CO_2: Carbon dioxide, a gas that is present in small amounts in the air. Plants need it in order to breathe.

coelacanth: A kind of lobe-finned fish (an ancient group of fish that includes the ancestor of four-legged animals). One kind of coelacanth is still alive today.

era: A very long amount of time in geological history that includes several periods. The dinosaurs all lived in the Mesozoic era.

formation: A set of rock layers that is distinct from the rocks above and below it.

fossil: Remains or traces of ancient living things. Most are turned to or encased in stone.

fungus: (plural: fungi) The group that includes mushrooms, yeast, and molds. Fungi do not photosynthesize and cannot make their own food from scratch the way plants can.

ginkgo: An ancient non-flowering tree with a characteristic fan-shaped leaf.

gut: The stomach and intestines of an animal.

horsetail: An ancient kind of nonflowering plant that still grows in damp places today.

invertebrate: An animal without a backbone.

larva: (plural: larvae) The first stage in the life of certain animals. Larvae may look very different from the adult animal. Mosquitoes and frogs start out as larvae.

lungfish: A kind of lobe-finned fish (see "coelacanth"). A few kinds of lungfish have survived to this day.

microbe: A microbe is the same thing as a microorganism.

microorganism: A life-form so small it can be seen only with the help of a microscope.

mites: Small relatives of spiders and ticks.

molecule: Two or more atoms that are stuck together and form the building blocks of most matter. A water molecule, for example, contains one oxygen atom and two hydrogen atoms.

mosasaurs: Giant predatory sea reptiles with big heads that were related to lizards and snakes.

nutrients: Things that plants and animals need to live and grow, such as fats, proteins, carbohydrates, and minerals.

paleo: Ancient. Adding "paleo-" in front of a word means that the word has to do with things that are ancient.

parasite: A plant or animal that lives on or in another living being and feeds off its host, often harming it in the process.

period: A chunk of time in geological history of roughly 50 million years, though some periods are quite a bit shorter or longer than that. The dinosaurs all lived in the Triassic, Jurassic, and Cretaceous periods of the Mesozoic era.

plesiosaurs: Sea reptiles with wide bodies and short tails.

pollinate: To take pollen from the flowers or cones of one plant to those of another plant so the plant can reproduce. Insects are important pollinators.

predator: An animal that hunts other animals for food.

prey: An animal that is hunted by other animals.

pterosaur: An extinct flying relative of the dinosaurs that had wings made of skin.

raptor: A bird of prey. Also used informally to refer to small and medium-size predatory dinosaurs such as *Velociraptor* and *Deinonychus*.

scavenger: An animal that eats dead animals that it did not kill.

Index

Thank-yous

First of all, many thanks and a round of applause for the scientists who agreed to be interviewed and who provided me with information and guidance. They are, in order of appearance: Karen Chin, curator of paleontology at the Museum of Natural History at the University of Colorado in Boulder; Paul Barrett, dinosaur researcher and curator at the Natural History Museum in London; Nizar Ibrahim, paleontologist at the University of Chicago and National Geographic Explorer; Carole Gee, professor and researcher at the University of Bonn in Germany; Conrad Labandeira, researcher and curator of fossil arthropods at the National Museum of Natural History in Washington, D.C.; and a strawberry plant with zero institutional affiliation but with lots of photosynthesis expertise.

Several other scientists contributed their knowledge and advice from behind the scenes: many thanks to Corwin Sullivan, Cindy Looy, Ivo Duijnstee, and Carl Mehling. Thanks also to schoolteacher extraordinaire Lyn Maslow, librarian Lisa Whip, and their students at the West Homer Elementary School in Homer, Alaska, for their help; to Alicia Ramis for her perspective as a biology teacher; and to fellow illustrator Flavia Gargiulo for her excellent visual input.

Warmest thanks also to my family and friends for their constant support and helpful suggestions. Last, but not least, a huge thanks to the team at National Geographic Books. I was lucky enough to work (again!) with master designer David Seager, and I received invaluable feedback and support from editors Shelby Alinsky and Paige Towler. Thanks also to the rest of the staff who were part of the making of the book.

Selected author's sources for text and images

Books

Barrett, Paul. *National Geographic Dinosaurs*. Washington, D.C.: National Geographic, 2001.

Fastovsky, David E., and David B. Weishampel. *Dinosaurs: A Concise Natural History*. 2nd ed. Cambridge: Cambridge University Press, 2012.

Paul, Gregory S. *The Princeton Field Guide to Dinosaurs*. Princeton, N.J.: Princeton University Press, 2010.

Articles

Barrett, Paul M. "The Diet of Ostrich Dinosaurs (Theropoda: Ornithomimosauria)." *Paleontology* 48 (2005): 347-58.

Chin, Karen. "The Paleobiological Implications of Herbivorous Dinosaur Coprolites From the Upper Cretaceous Two Medicine Formation of Montana: Why Eat Wood?" *Palaios* 22, no. 5 (2007): 554-66.

Chin, Karen, and Bruce D. Gill. "Dinosaurs, Dung Beetles, and Conifers: Participants in a Cretaceous Food Web." *Palaios* 11 (1996): 280-85.

DePalma, Robert A., David A. Burnham, Larry D. Martin, Bruce M. Rothschild, and Peter L. Larson. "Physical Evidence of a Predatory Behaviour in *Tyrannosaurus rex*." *Proceedings of the National Academy of Sciences of the United States of America* 110, no. 31 (2013): 12560-64.

Hummel, Jürgen, Carole T. Gee, Karl-Heinz Südekum, Martin P. Sander, Gunther Nogge, and Marcus Clauss. "In Vitro Digestibility of Fern and Gymnosperm Foliage: Implications for Sauropod Feeding Ecology and Diet Selection." *Proceedings, Biological Sciences/The Royal Society* 275, no. 1638 (2008): 1015-21.

Ibrahim, Nizar, Paul C. Sereno, Cristiano Dal Sasso, Simone Maganuco, Matteo Fabbri, David M. Martill, Samir Zouhri, Nathan Myhrvold, and Dawid A. Iurino. "Semiaquatic Adaptations in a Giant Predatory Dinosaur." *Science* 345, no. 6204 (2014): 1613-16.

Labandeira, Conrad C., Peter Wilf, and Kirk R. Johnson. "Guide to Insect (and Other) Damage Types on Compressed Plant Fossils." Version 3.0. Washington, D.C.: Smithsonian Institution, 2007.

O'Connor, Jingmai, Zhonghe Zhou, and Xing Xu. "Additional Specimen of Microraptor Provides Unique Evidence of Dinosaurs Preying on Birds." *Proceedings of the National Academy of Sciences of the United States of America* 108, no. 49 (2011): 19662-65.

Pott, Christian, Stephen McLoughlin, Anders Lindström, Shunqing Wu, and Else Marie Friis. "*Baikalophyllum lobatum* and *Rehezamites anisolobus*: Two Seed Plants With 'Cycadophyte' Foliage From the Early Cretaceous of Eastern Asia." *International Journal of Plant Sciences* 173 (2012): 192-208.

Sullivan, Corwin, David W. E. Hone, Xing Xu, and Fucheng Zhang. "The Asymmetry of the Carpal Joint and the Evolution of Wing Folding in Maniraptoran Theropod Dinosaurs." *Proceedings, Biological Sciences/The Royal Society* 277, no. 1690 (2010): 2027-33.

Wang, Xiaolin, Rui Pan, Richard J. Butler, and Paul M. Barrett. "The Postcranial Skeleton of the Iguanodontian Ornithopod *Jinzhousaurus yangi* From the Lower Cretaceous Yixian Formation of Western Liaoning, China." *Earth and Environmental Science Transactions of the Royal Society of Edinburgh* 101 (2010): 135-159.

Wings, Oliver, and P. Martin Sander. "No Gastric Mill in Sauropod Dinosaurs: New Evidence From Analysis of Gastrolith Mass and Function in Ostriches." *Proceedings, Biological Sciences/The Royal Society* 274, no. 1610 (2007): 635-40.

Xing, Lida, W. Scott Persons, Phil R. Bell, Xing Xu, Jianping Zhang, Tetsuto Miyashita, Fengping Wang, and Philip J. Currie. "Piscivory in the Feathered Dinosaur Microraptor." *Evolution* 67, no. 8 (2013): 2441-45.

Zhou, Zhonghe. "The Jehol Biota, an Early Cretaceous Terrestrial Lagerstatte: New Discoveries and Implications." *National Science Review* 1, no. 4 (2014): 543-59.

Websites

Jason Brougham Paleontological Art, jasonbrougham.com

Scott Hartman's Skeletal Drawing.com, skeletaldrawing.com

The Paleobiota of the Yixian Formation on Wikipedia, wikipedia.org

Countless image searches, photos of fossils, and reconstructions of animals, plants, and environments, including those of Jason Brougham, Brian Choo, John Conway, and many more

To Lily, Leo, and Adèle, who share my love of drawing.

Since 1888, the National Geographic Society has funded more than 12,000 research, exploration, and preservation projects around the world. The Society receives funds from National Geographic Partners LLC, funded in part by your purchase. A portion of the proceeds from this book supports this vital work. To learn more, visit www.natgeo.com/info.

For more information, visit www.nationalgeographic.com, call 1-800-647-5463, or write to the following address:

National Geographic Partners
1145 17th Street N.W.
Washington, D.C. 20036-4688 U.S.A.

Visit us online at www.nationalgeographic.com/books

For librarians and teachers: www.ngchildrensbooks.org

More for kids from National Geographic: kids.nationalgeographic.com

For information about special discounts for bulk purchases, please contact National Geographic Books Special Sales: ngspecsales@ngs.org

For rights or permissions inquiries, please contact National Geographic Books Subsidiary Rights: ngbooksrights@ngs.org

Designed by David M. Seager
The text is set in Billy.

Hardcover ISBN: 978-1-4263-2339-3
Reinforced library binding ISBN: 978-1-4263-2340-9

Printed in Hong Kong
16/THK/1